WHAT'S UP, DOC?

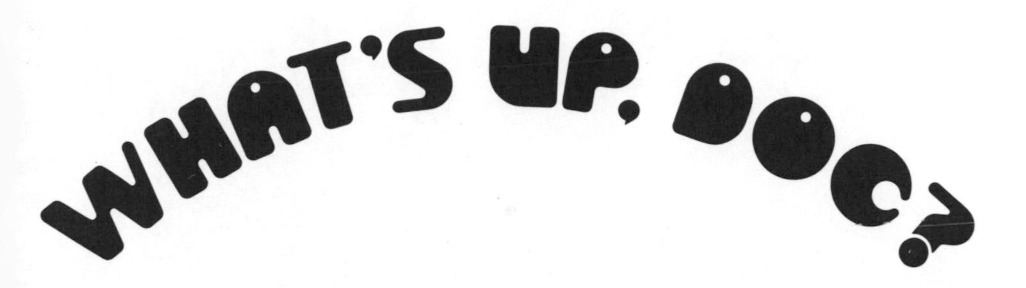

DOCTOR & DENTIST JOKES

Compiled by Charles Keller
Illustrated by Leonard Kessler

Prentice-Hall, Inc., Englewood Cliffs, New Jersey

Printed in the United States of America •J

Prentice-Hall International, Inc., London
Prentice-Hall of Australia, Pty. Ltd., Sydney
Prentice-Hall Canada, Inc., Toronto
Prentice-Hall of India Private Ltd., New Delhi
Prentice-Hall of Japan, Inc., Tokyo
Prentice-Hall of Southeast Asia Pte. Ltd., Singapore
Whitehall Books Limited, Wellington, New Zealand
Editora Prentice-Hall do Brasil LTDA., Rio de Janeiro

10 9 8 7 6 5 4 3 2

Library of Congress Cataloging in Publication Data

Keller, Charles.
What's up doc?

Summary: A collection of jokes about doctors and dentists including "What did the surgeon say to the uncooperative patient?—Suture self," and "Doctor, what does it mean when someone has tiny pupils?—It could mean she's a kindergarten teacher."

1. Medicine—Anecdotes, facetiae, satire, etc. 2. Wit and humor, Juvenile. [1. Medicine—Wit and humor. 2. Jokes] I. Kessler, Leonard P., 1920– , ill. II. Title.
PN6231.M4K4 1984 818'.5402 84-6821

For Barbara, Carol, and Connie

Honey, the doctor is here.
Tell him I can't see him, I'm sick.

Are you taking care of your cold?
I've had it for weeks and it seems as good as new.

Doctor, I think I've lost my memory.
How long has this been going on?
How long has what been going on?

Who wrote, "Oh, Say, Can You See?"
An eye doctor?

I was just bitten on the leg by a dog.
Did you put anything on it?
No, he liked it just the way it was.

What's the best way to prevent infection caused by biting insects?
Don't bite any.

Your leg is swollen, but I wouldn't worry about it.
If your leg was swollen, I wouldn't worry about it either.

I hear you take milk baths. How come?
I can't find a cow tall enough for a shower.

Good morning, doctor, I just dropped in to tell you how much I benefited from your treatment.
But you're not one of my patients.
I know. But my uncle Harry was and I'm his heir.

Doctor, I have this terrible pain in my back.
Did you ever have it before?
Yes, several times.
Well, it looks like you've got it again.

That's a bad cut you have on your head. How did you get it?
I bit myself.
How could you bite yourself on the head?
I stood on a chair.

Who is the most famous baby doctor?
I didn't know babies were doctors.

Did you hear about the outbreak of Russian measles?
No. What's it like?
Instead of breaking out in little red circles, you break out in red squares.

On my first visit here you told me to take one pill, skip an hour, then take another one.
Did you follow my instructions?
No, after skipping for an hour I was too tired to take the second pill.

Why didn't the lady want the doctor to operate on her husband?
Because she didn't want anyone to open her male.

What two letters do teeth hate most?
D – K.

What's the condition of the boy who swallowed the quarter?
No change yet.

Doctor, I think corn is growing out of my ears.
Why, so it is. How did this happen?
Beats me—I planted radishes.

I'm the doctor's nurse.
Oh, is the doctor sick?

I will examine you for twenty dollars.
Go ahead, Doc. If you find it, you can have it.

Stick out your tongue.
What for? I'm not mad at you.

I'll take another bottle of that cough medicine.
You must have a bad cough.
No, I like it on my pancakes.

You can mix this medicine with orange juice so you won't taste it.
Good, I don't like the taste of orange juice.

I laughed after my operation.
How come?
The doctor had me in stitches.

I wanted to be a tree surgeon but I changed my mind.
How come?
I couldn't stand the sight of sap.

What are the words in a dentist's office that can make the pain go away?
"You're next."

I've been operating for years and never had a single complaint.
Sure. How many talking horses are there?

My grandmother's hard of hearing and the doctor said he could operate to help her hear better.
What did she say?
She said she was 90 years old and had heard enough.

I started sleeping with my bicycle last night.
Why?
I got tired of sleep walking.

What do you call an operation on a rabbit?
A hare-cut.

Nurse, ask the patient his name so we can notify his family.
The patient says his family already knows his name.

Well, doc, how do I stand?
That's what I'd like to know.

Billy, why didn't you tell me your stomach hurt?
Aw, Mom, I figured you would just think I was bellyaching.

What do you get when you cross a cold with a leaky faucet?
Cough drops.

I was seeing fuzzy spots before my eyes, so I got a pair of glasses.
Did they help?
Sure did. I see the spots much clearer now.

Good grief, you've got the biggest cavity I've ever seen. Ever seen. Ever seen.
You don't have to repeat yourself.
I didn't. That was an echo.

What did the surgeon say to the uncooperative patient?
Suture self.

I think you should take something for that cold.
Oh, good, I'll take the rest of the week off.

My chiropractor is upset.
How come?
He says he gets nothing but back talk.

That's some cold you've got. What are you taking for it?
I don't know. How much will you give me?

My doctor says exercise will kill germs.
But how can you get them to exercise?

Why do you look over your glasses instead of through them?
So I won't wear them out.

Doctor, you've got to help me. My head feels like a piece of iron, my throat feels like a rusty pipe, and my nose keeps running like a faucet.
You don't need me, you need a plumber.

Doctor, do you think oysters are healthy?
I never knew one that complained.

Doctor, I feel like I'm on pins and needles.
Then you'd better stand up. That's my nurse's sewing you're sitting on.

My veterinarian has a sore throat.
Of course. He's a hoarse doctor.

Doc, I need help. I think I'm a dog.
Please come into the office and sit down.
I can't do that. I'm not allowed on the furniture.

I didn't sleep very well last night.
Why not?
I plugged my electric blanket into the toaster and kept popping out of bed all night.

How many bones do you have in your body?
One thousand.
That's more than anyone else.
I had fish for lunch.

Doctor, what does it mean when someone has tiny pupils?
It could mean that she's a kindergarten teacher.

Oh! Ouch!
I haven't even started yet.
I know. I'm just practicing.

Doc, you pulled the wrong tooth.
Don't worry, I'm coming to it.

Stop yelling. I haven't even put the needle in yet.
I know, but you're standing on my foot.

Do you suffer from arthritis?
Sure, what else can you do with it?

What do you mean, you have a religious headache?
My temples hurt.

Today we will discuss the heart, lungs, and liver.
Just another organ recital.

How do you want your medicine?
With a fork.

How long can you live without a brain, Doc?
I don't know. How old are you?

My father is in the hospital.
I'm sorry to hear that. Is he sick?
No. He's a doctor.

My aunt went to Arizona for her asthma.
Why? Couldn't she get it here?

I just completed my 2,000th successful operation.
How did you accomplish such a remarkable feat?
It took a lot of patients.

I'm really worried about my brother. He thinks he's an elevator.
I'll have to look at him. Send him up.
I can't. He doesn't stop on your floor.

I've examined you thoroughly. I think all you need is a rest.
But I feel sick. Why don't you look at my tongue?
It needs a rest, too.

Doc, is it true that large doses of vitamin C can cure the common cold?
It's only a theory but I have patients who think so.
Do they ever complain of colds?
I don't know. After they've sucked twenty lemons a day, you can't understand them.

Don't you think it's terrible when a doctor puts that stick in your mouth?
Yes, it's really depressing.

Doctor, you're great! My back pain is completely gone. What was the trouble, rheumatism?
No, your suspenders were twisted.

Your son had only one cavity.
That's great. How did he do it?
He has only one tooth.

Doctor, I have water on the knee. What should I do?
Wear pumps.

Why are you jumping up and down like that?
The doctor gave me some medicine and I forgot to shake the bottle.

Is your cold positive or negative?
What do you mean?
Do the eyes have it or the nose?

I just got this new hearing aid. It's the best one on the market.
What kind is it?
Oh, it's half past four.

Do you drink plenty of liquids?
Yes, doctor, that's all I drink.

How can I get to the nearest hospital fast?
Just stand in the middle of that street.

Doc, there's something wrong with my stomach.
Keep your shirt buttoned and no one will notice it.

You look better today. Did the medicine help?
Yes, Doc, I followed the directions on the bottle.
What were they?
Keep the bottle tightly closed.

Mother, that dentist wasn't painless as he advertised.

Why, did he hurt you?

No, but he yelled just like the others when I bit his finger.

Are you sure one bottle of this will cure a cold?
It must. Nobody ever came back for a second bottle.

Have your eyes ever been checked?
No, they were always brown.

Doctor, every bone in my body hurts. What should I do?
Be glad you're not a fish.

Doc, my rabbit is sick and I can't understand it. I feed it nothing but goat's milk.
Goat's milk, eh. That's the problem. You're not supposed to use that greasy kid stuff on your hare.

Why does a doctor wear a mask during operations?
If something goes wrong, nobody can identify him.

You should cut out those pills. They could be habit-forming.
Don't be silly. I've been taking them for ten years now.

I'm sorry I made you wait so long.
Oh, I didn't mind the wait so much, but I thought you'd like to treat my ailment in its early stages.

Doc, I hate to bother you at 3 A.M., but I have a bad case of insomnia.
Well, what are you trying to do, start an epidemic?

My brother thinks he's a chicken and keeps clucking all day.
Why don't you take him to a doctor?
I did, but he was a quack.

What kind of filling do you want in your tooth?
Chocolate.

Doctor, my husband thinks he's a parking meter.
That's serious. Have him come to see me this Friday.
Sorry, he can't. Friday is the day they come and take the coins out of his mouth.

Doctor, you charged me $15 and all you did was paint my throat.
What did you expect, wallpaper?

Doctor, I think I'm becoming a highway.
What's come over you?
So far two trucks, one bus, six cars, and a motorcycle.

My dentist lost his glasses.
That's terrible.
I know. He'd give his eyeteeth to have them back.

Doc, that ointment you gave me makes my arm smart.
In that case, rub some on your head.

You have to stop worrying and thinking about yourself so much. Throw yourself into your work.
But, Doc, I run a cement mixer.

Doc, I have a sore throat.
Go over to my window and stick out your tongue.
Why, will you be able to see better over there?
No, I don't like my neighbors.

Have you made any progress since you first came to me and told me you kept thinking you were a dog?
A little. I've stopped chasing cars.

I've got a pain in my left foot.
It's nothing to worry about. It's just old age.
Then why doesn't my right foot hurt too? I've had it just as long.

Doctor, my foot falls asleep and wakes me up.
If your foot falls asleep, why does it wake you up?
It snores.

My brother is in the hospital with a broken leg. I wonder what I should get him as a present.
Anything at all. He won't kick.

How can you avoid falling hair, Doc?
Jump out of the way.

Doctor, I just swallowed a harmonica. What should I do?
Keep calm and be happy.
Happy? About what?
That you weren't playing the piano.

My father's been in the hospital for several weeks now.
Flu, I suppose?
Yes, and crashed.

Doctor, what causes baldness?
Lack of hair.

Tell me about your dreams this last week.
I didn't dream at all this week.
I can't help you if you don't do your homework.

My brother swallowed a frog.
Did it make him sick?
Yes, he's liable to croak any minute.

How do you know carrots are good for the eyes?
You never saw a rabbit wearing glasses, did you?

You've got to help me, Doctor. My wife thinks she's a pretzel.
Bring her in to see me. Maybe I can straighten her out.

Doctor, I need more of those iron pills you gave me.
Why?
I left them out in the rain and they rusted.

Tell me, Doctor, what do you think of artificial respiration?
I'd rather have the real thing.

Do you find it hard to make decisions?
Well—yes and no.

What would you do if you had rabies?
I'd ask for a pen and paper.
To make out a will?
No, to make a list of people I'd bite.

Don't you know that my hours are from 2 P.M. to 4 P.M.?
Yes, but the dog that bit me didn't.

Doctor, how much do you charge to extract a tooth?
Twenty dollars.
What? Twenty dollars for only five minutes' work?
If you wish, I can extract the tooth very slowly.

Doctor, I'll open my mouth very, very wide.
Madam, you don't have to open that wide. I plan to stand outside.

Doc, I just broke my arm in four places. What can I do?
Stay out of those places.

On this diet you can eat anything you like.
That's great.
Now here's a list of things you're going to like.

Hello, is this the acupuncturist who treated me this afternoon? The pain is still there.
Take two pins and call me in the morning.

What kind of work do you do?
I work on a farm detasseling corn.
But aren't you allergic to corn?
Yes, but $5 an hour is nothing to sneeze at.

Did you ever have an accident?
No, but a rattlesnake once bit me.
Don't you call that an accident?
Of course not. He did it on purpose.

Doctor, my baby swallowed a bullet. What should I do?

Don't point him at anybody.

Doctor, don't you think you overcharged me for taking care of my daughter when she had the measles?
Remember, I had to make five house calls.
Yes, but she infected the whole school, and look how much business that brought you.

Tell me, doctor, can an eight-year-old take out a person's appendix?
Of course not.
You hear that, Johnny? Go put it back.

I just called to make an appointment with the dentist.
The dentist is out at the moment. Can you call back?
Sure. When do you expect him to be out again?

Doctor, you have to do something for me. I snore so loud I wake myself up.
Then I advise you to sleep in another room.

Where does a sick boat go?
Straight to the dock.

Did you hear about the guy who accidently cut off his left side?
He's all right now.

I'm afraid you have canary disease.
Can you cure me, doc?
Yes, it's tweetable.

Where does an Egyptian go when he has a bad back?
To the Cairo-practor.

Why are you in such a hurry to have me cure your cold?
I lost my handkerchief.

Do you use toothpaste?
What for? My teeth aren't loose.

I'm having trouble chewing with my teeth.
You'd have more trouble chewing without them.

Are you sure you want 50 quarts of milk?
Yes, my doctor told me to take a bath in milk.
Do you want it pasteurized?
No, just up to my chin.

My uncle Henry wanted a brain transplant.
No kidding! What happened to him?
Fortunately, the doctors were able to change his mind.

I just swallowed a great big bug.
Shouldn't you take something for it?
No, I'll just let it starve.

My doctor told me my husband needed fresh mountain air.
Did you take him to the mountains?
No. But I fanned him every night with a picture of the Alps.

Doctor, my brother is crazy. He thinks he's Napoleon, but he can't be.
Why not?
Because I am.

Doc, my son swallowed the film from my camera.
Don't worry. Nothing will develop.

Doctor, I've had two dimes stuck in my ear since last year.
Why didn't you come and see me sooner?
I didn't need the money until now.

Doctor, I can't sleep at night.
Why not?
I sleep with my sister and she thinks she's a refrigerator.
How does that keep you awake?
She sleeps with her mouth open and the little light keeps me awake.

My doctor says I have mumps. What should I do?
Have a swell time.

Doctor, how can I live to be 100 years old?
Eat an apple a day for 36,500 days.

Why did the optometrist move to Alaska?
Because he wanted to be an optical Aleutian.

What's a dentist's favorite song?
Leader of the Plaque.

How do I avoid getting that run-down feeling?
Look both ways before crossing the street.

My grandfather was 85 and never needed glasses.
Lots of people drink from the bottle.

Doctor, why did you charge me double for pulling my son's tooth?
He yelled so loud he chased away the other patients.

Where were you born?
In a hospital.
No kidding. What was wrong with you?

The doctor gave me some medicine and told me to take three teaspoonfuls after every meal.
Did you?
No, we only have two teaspoons.

Does your dentist have an electric toothbrush?
No, none of his patients have electric teeth.

Did you follow my instructions and drink water thirty minutes before going to bed?
I tried to, Doc, but I was completely full after drinking for only five minutes.

I just had my appendix removed.
Have a scar?
No, thanks. I don't smoke.

I hope your dog doesn't have fleas.
Why, Doctor?
I don't like starting from scratch.

I got my head stuck in the washing machine.
Were you hurt?
No, but I got brainwashed.

First I had tonsillitis, followed by appendicitis and pneumonia, ending with neuritis. Then they gave me hypodermic and inoculation.
Boy, did you have a hard time!
I'll say. I never thought I'd pass that spelling test.

Last night I couldn't get to sleep so I tried counting sheep. I counted up to 30,000.
Then did you get to sleep?
No, by then it was time to get up.

What seems to be your trouble?
It's my head. I've had it on and off for several days now.

You cough more easily now.
I should. I've been practicing all night.

Doctor, I keep thinking I'm a horse.
Well, I can cure you, but it will cost a lot of money.
Money's no problem. I won the Kentucky Derby last week.

My feet hurt.
Why don't you soak them in hot water?
What? And get my shoes all wet?

Did you have a good time at the dentist?
No, I was bored to tears.

How did you have this accident?
The sign said, STOP LOOK LISTEN! But while I did, the train hit me.

Doc, I'm afraid I'm going to die.
Nonsense. That's the last thing you'll do.

Something is wrong with me, Doc. I keep thinking I'm a dog.
How long has this been going on?
Since I was a puppy.

Are you taking your medicine regularly?
No, Doc, I tasted it and decided to keep on coughing.

I wish the doctor would hurry up and call me.
Be a little patient.
I am one.

What makes you think our dentist is moody?
He always looks down in the mouth.

Mr. Johnson, I think you're suffering from a split personality.
No, we aren't.

I had to go to the dentist today.
Does your tooth still hurt?
I don't know—the dentist kept it.

Did that new weight loss diet help your sister?
It sure did. Last week she completely disappeared.

How did you sleep last night?
As usual, with my eyes closed.

Nobody lives forever.
Mind if I try, Doc?

Some doctors say that ten years from now, measles will be unknown.
What a rash prediction.